Happy F Friends

Friends

HAMSTERS

Written by Izzi Howell
Illustrated by Charlotte Cotterill

D1628416

C334823485

First published in Great Britain in 2022 by Wayland
Copyright © Hodder and Stoughton, 2022

Produced for Wayland by
White-Thomson Publishing Ltd
www.wtpub.co.uk

HB ISBN: 978 1 5263 1687 5   PB ISBN: 978 1 5263 1688 2

Credits
Author and editor: Izzi Howell
Illustrator: Charlotte Cotterill
Designer: Clare Nicholas
Cover designer: Ellie Boultwood
Proofreader: Annabel Savery

Picture credits: Alamy: Papilio 18; Getty: Kerrick 7b, greg801 8, trgowanlock 11t, Ihar Halavach 15, LightFieldStudios 23, Natalia Duryagina 26; Shutterstock: Eric Isselee cover, title page and 19, Olesya Zhuk 4t, Olena Kurashova 4bl, 21 and 29, Viachaslau Kraskouski 4br, irin-k 5b, Clari Massimiliano 6t, Dmytro Leschenko 6b, Slim379 7t, Anton Starikov 9t and 28t, JessicaGirvan 9b, ifong 10l, Natalia7 10r, Einar Arnason 11b, Kristi Blokhin 12, stock_shot 13, Mary Swift 14, elladoro 16, Richard Peterson 17l, Ostanina Ekaterina 17r, tanya_morozz 20, Oleksandr Lytvynenko 22 and 28b, Kryazheva Alena 24, haveseen 25, Lepas 27.

All design elements from Shutterstock.

The website addresses (URLs) included in this book were valid at the time of going to press. However, it is possible that contents or addresses may have changed since the publication of this book. No responsibility for any such changes can be accepted by either the author or the Publisher.

Printed and bound in China

Wayland, an imprint of
Hachette Children's Group
Part of Hodder and Stoughton
Carmelite House
50 Victoria Embankment
London EC4Y 0DZ

An Hachette UK Company
www.hachettechildrens.co.uk

Contents

The Perfect Pet

Hamsters can make perfect pets!
They are cute, fun and friendly.
But having a hamster is a **BIG**
responsibility. You need
to take **SPECIAL CARE**
of hamsters, because
they can get hurt or
scared easily.

A hamster is covered
in *soft, fuzzy fur*.

Can you spot your
hamster's *teeny, tiny tail*?

MOST HAMSTERS KEPT AS PETS ARE SYRIAN HAMSTERS.

**Your Syrian hamster
must be kept alone
because it won't like
sharing its space with
other hamsters.**

Syrian hamsters are also called **golden hamsters**,
even though they come in lots of different colours!

Hamsters listen to what's going on with their **sensitive ears**.

Hamsters don't have very good *eyesight*.

Their **whiskers** help hamsters to find their way around.

A hamster has **four small feet** with **sharp claws** for digging.

Furry Friend FACT!

A hamster's whiskers can vibrate backwards and forwards up to 30 times a second! Hamsters move their sensitive whiskers to explore their environment and feel what's around them.

Most Syrian hamsters have **short hair**, but a few types have **long hair**.

Dwarf Hamster Duos

Siberian dwarf hamster

Dwarf hamsters are another common type of hamster. These **POCKET-SIZED PETS** are much smaller than Syrian hamsters. But like Syrian hamsters, they come in many colours!

The winter white dwarf hamster (also called the Russian dwarf hamster) has brown and white fur.

Furry Friend FACT!

The smallest breed of pet hamster is the Roborovski dwarf hamster. Adults are only 4–5 cm long, which is about the same size as a kiwi fruit!

AS BIG AS A KIWI AND JUST AS SWEET!

Unlike Syrian hamsters, dwarf hamsters can be happy housemates! They can be kept in **PAIRS** or **THREES**. However, you must make sure their cage is large enough for all of them.

THREE TIMES THE CUTENESS!

Dwarf hamsters can be best buddies if they are kept together from a young age. If you try to introduce them at an older age, fights can happen.

Home Sweet Home

Pet hamsters need to live indoors in a cage. Make sure there are no gaps in or sharp edges on the bars. Hamsters need lots of **SPACE** to **MOVE** and **PLAY**, so the bigger the cage the better!

This multi-layer cage gives your hamster more room to play.

Hamsters love climbing up wire bars!

The cage should have a deep plastic base so that there is enough room for litter.

THEY CALL ME HAIRY HOUDINI!

Furry Friend FACT!

Hamsters are escape artists and will squeeze out of their cage if the bars are too wide apart! Be aware that tiny dwarf hamsters can fit through even smaller gaps than their bigger cousins.

Fill the bottom of the cage with litter, such as **DUST-FREE WOOD SHAVINGS** or **CORN COB GRANULES**. Don't use straw, as this can cut your hamster's cheek pouches. Make the litter as **DEEP** as possible, so that your hamster can dig and burrow.

Your hamster needs a **NESTING BOX** to sleep in. Make it **COSY** by filling it with nesting materials such as hay, shredded paper or cardboard.

dust-free wood shavings

Choose a nesting box without a base. This will allow you to pick the box up to check on your hamster while it's snoozing if you need to!

ZZZZZZZ

Peace and Quiet

As well as a cosy cage, your hamster needs to live in the perfect spot. Its cage must be in a **WARM, DRY PLACE**. It shouldn't be in direct sunlight or your hamster will get too hot and sweaty!

Hamsters are very **SENSITIVE** to a type of noise called **ULTRASOUND** that comes from household appliances, such as computers and TVs. We can't hear ultrasound, but hamsters can. It hurts their ears if they hear it a lot, so they need to be kept away from ultrasound sources.

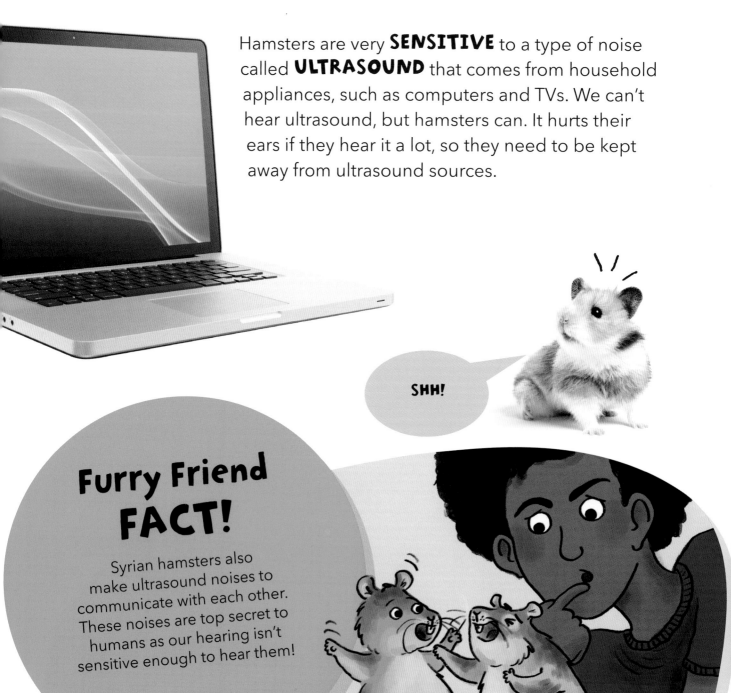

SHH!

Furry Friend FACT!

Syrian hamsters also make ultrasound noises to communicate with each other. These noises are top secret to humans as our hearing isn't sensitive enough to hear them!

NIGHT TIME IS PLAY TIME!

Hamster play time is during the night. You shouldn't wake up your hamster to play during the day, as this will make it feel stressed.

Hamsters are **NOCTURNAL**, which means that they **SNOOZE** for most of the day and party all night long! Your hamster's cage needs to be in a place where your hamster can **REST QUIETLY** during the day, and won't keep you up at night when it is being **NOISY**.

Nourishing Nibbles

Your hamster needs a balanced diet to stay healthy. You can either buy ready-made hamster mix or give your hamster a range of different foods, including yummy **SEEDS, GRAINS, NUTS, GREEN VEGETABLES** and **FRUIT**. Never give your hamster grapes or rhubarb, as they are poisonous for hamsters.

Make sure your hamster can always reach its water in a valveless drinking bottle in case it gets thirsty. Change the water once a day.

GLUG, GLUG, GLUG!

You can feed your hamster in its own bowl or on the floor of the cage, but it probably won't eat there! Hamsters have large **POUCHES** (pockets) inside their **CHEEKS**. They grab lots of food and carry it in their pouches to private spaces where they feel **SAFE**, such as their nesting box, where they can eat in peace and quiet.

You may spot your hamster with mega cheeks bulging with lots of yummy snacks for later!

Furry Friend FACT!

Syrian hamsters can hold up to half their body weight in food in their cheek pouches.

Handle with Care

Hamsters are shy animals. In the wild, they are the prey of many bigger predators, so pet hamsters are naturally **SCARED** of larger animals, including you!

Humans are also much **BIGGER** than hamsters. Being picked up by a human probably feels a bit like if you were scooped up and stroked by a **GIANT!** Handling your hamster **GENTLY** and **CALMLY** will help it to stay calm.

Wait for your hamster to wake up naturally before touching it. If you handle it while it is sleeping, you may get bitten. Ouch!

READY TO PLAY!

To **HANDLE** a hamster safely, **CUP** it with both hands. Then open up your hands and let the hamster **EXPLORE** them slowly. **ALWAYS** hold the hamster close to a surface in case it makes a sudden jump!

Handling your hamster at the same time every day will help it to feel more relaxed.

Furry Friend FACT!

Hamsters can easily break a bone if they fall from a height or get their legs caught in their cage bars. You must be very careful when handling them.

Gnawing Gnashers

Hamsters' teeth **NEVER** stop growing. They need to **GNAW** things to keep their teeth short and sharp. If their teeth get too long, it can make them **ILL** and stop them from eating properly. If you notice your hamster looking a bit too **TOOTHY**, take it to the vet for a tooth trim!

CHECK OUT MY CHOPPERS!

This hamster has short teeth, which are perfect for munching on tasty treats.

The best **CHEW TOYS** for hamsters are **NATURAL WOODEN TOYS** or special gnawing branches from a pet shop. Chewing other things, such as the metal bars of their cage, can **HURT** their teeth.

This wooden toy from a pet shop is perfect for gnawing!

This hamster is munching on a wooden chew toy.

WHAT SHARP TEETH YOU'VE GOT ...

Furry Friend FACT!

Hamsters' teeth sharpen themselves. Their front teeth rub against each other while they are gnawing, acting as a natural sharpener.

Keeping Clean

It may not be your favourite job, but it's very **IMPORTANT** to keep your hamster's cage clean. Change the water, food, litter and bedding **REGULARLY**. Don't let litter or bedding become damp or smelly. You also need to **CLEAN** the base of the cage with a **PET-SAFE CLEANER** once a week.

Keeping your hamster's cage clean will help your hamster to stay happy and healthy!

However, cleaning **TOO MUCH** can make your hamster **STRESSED** and **CONFUSED**. To keep your hamster calm during cleaning, put everything back in the same place. Clean the cage in the **EVENING** while your hamster is awake.

Keep back a small amount of **USED** nesting material that is clean and dry and put it in with the **NEW** material. The **SMELL** of the used nesting material will make your hamster feel at **HOME!**

Don't worry about washing your hamster — it washes itself! If your hamster stops grooming itself, it might mean that it's sick.

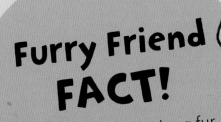

Furry Friend FACT!

If your hamster has long fur, you may need to groom it with a special brush. Ask your vet to recommend one.

Happy Hamster Toys

A happy hamster is a healthy hamster!
They love to **PLAY** and have fun with
different **TOYS**. One of the best
toys for hamsters is a **TUBE**.
They love squeeeeezing
through it!

If you have room, your hamster may enjoy a
long, complex tube system. Keep an eye on the
open ends of the tube so it doesn't escape!

A **RUNNING WHEEL** is also a good toy for hamsters. It provides good **EXERCISE** inside their cage. Make sure you buy the biggest wheel possible. Your hamster's back should not be bent while **RUNNING** in the wheel, as this can hurt it.

YOU CAN'T CATCH ME!

Hamster wheels should be solid (not wire). Otherwise, their tiny feet can get caught while running at top speed.

Furry Friend FACT!

Syrian hamsters can run up to 9 km in a night! This distance is almost the same as the height of Mount Everest!

Safety First

Your hamster will have fun spending time **OUTSIDE** its cage, but you must make sure it stays **SAFE**. Never leave your hamster alone! Hamsters are excellent at **HIDE-AND-SEEK** and it will take you a long time to find one.

I'M A NAUGHTY NIBBLER!

Never let your hamster nibble electrical cables as it may get a nasty shock.

Furry Friend FACT!

If your hamster does escape, one good way to track it down is to turn off the lights and listen carefully. You'll probably hear it gnawing on snacks from its cheek pouches!

Keep your hamster **AWAY** from any other pets, even well-behaved ones. Larger animals are hamsters' predators and they will make the hamster feel **FRIGHTENED**. Worst case scenario – your pets could hurt or kill the hamster accidentally, or on purpose.

Young children don't know how to touch hamsters gently and might hurt them. It's best for them to say hello to the hamster from a distance.

Is My Hamster Ill?

It's important to get to know your hamster's habits as any **CHANGES** to its normal **BEHAVIOUR** might mean that it is **ILL**. Look out for things like not eating or drinking as much, not keeping themselves clean, runny poo or sneezing a lot … **ATCHOO!**

A healthy hamster has bright eyes and glossy fur. Check your hamster regularly for any lumps, bumps or problems with its legs.

A **HAPPY** hamster is never **BORED**. It's important to keep your hamster **ENTERTAINED** or it can become **STRESSED**. If your hamster starts running in circles or chewing the bars of the cage a lot, it might need more **SPACE** or more **TOYS**.

PEEK-A-BOO!

Hamsters don't need expensive toys. The inside of a toilet roll is lots of fun!

Furry Friend FACT!

Hamsters can catch colds from humans and become very ill. Don't handle your hamster if you have a cold.

A Trip to the Vet

You should always talk to the **VET** if you are worried about your hamster's **HEALTH**. It's also a good idea to take your hamster to the vet for a health check when you first bring it home, and then every **THREE** to **SIX** months as it gets older.

During a health check, the vet will check every part of your hamster from head to tail!

Vets don't usually **NEUTER** or **SPAY** hamsters as the operation is too stressful for them. Syrian hamsters live **ALONE**, so you don't need to worry about babies. But male and female dwarf hamsters should be kept apart to avoid any **SURPRISE** litters!

Syrian hamsters usually have about four to six babies in each litter.

ONE, TWO, THREE ... WHERE'S YOUR SISTER?!

Furry Friend FACT!

Syrian hamsters are only pregnant for around 16 days before giving birth.

Pet Pop Quiz

Test your hamster knowledge with this pop quiz! The more you know about your pet, the happier and healthier it will be in your care.

1

Which type of hamster must live alone?

2

What are good materials for your hamster's nesting box?

3

Why should your hamster's cage be kept far away from household appliances?

4

When are hamsters awake and active?

5

Which fruits are poisonous to hamsters?

6
How do hamsters carry food?

7
What are the best things for your hamster to gnaw on?

8
Why are solid hamster wheels recommended?

9
How often should you clean the base of your hamster's cage?

10
Why should you not handle your hamster if you have a cold?

HOW MANY DID YOU GET RIGHT?

Answers:
1. A Syrian hamster; 2. Hay, shredded paper or cardboard; 3. They make ultrasound noises that upset hamsters; 4. During the night; 5. Grapes and rhubarb; 6. In their cheek pouches; 7. Natural wooden toys or special gnawing branches; 8. Hamsters can trap and hurt their feet in wire wheels; 9. Once a week; 10. Your hamster can catch the cold and become very ill.

Glossary

breed one of many different types of animal of the same species

burrow to dig a hole in the ground; the underground home of an animal

gnaw to bite down on something to wear it away

groom to clean an animal's fur

litter all of the babies that an animal has at one time; material used to line the bottom of a cage

neuter to stop an animal from being able to have babies

nocturnal describes something that is awake during the night and asleep during the day

poisonous something that can be dangerous if eaten

predator an animal that hunts and eats other animals for food

prey an animal that is hunted and eaten by other animals

responsibility to be dependable, make good choices and take account of your actions, often for the good of something else

spay to stop a female animal from being able to have babies

ultrasound a type of noise produced by household appliances that humans can't hear, but some animals can

vet someone who gives animals medical care and treatment

BOOKS TO READ

My New Pet: Hamster and Gerbil by Jinny Johnson (Franklin Watts, 2015)

Pet Expert: Hamsters and Guinea Pigs by Gemma Barder (Wayland, 2020)

Pet Pals: Hamsters by Pat Jacobs (Wayland, 2018)

FURTHER INFORMATION

To find out more about hamsters and how you can look after your pet to keep it happy and healthy, you can visit these websites:

www.rspca.org.uk/adviceandwelfare/pets/rodents/hamsters
Find lots of information about your hamster's diet, cage and behaviour.

www.pdsa.org.uk/taking-care-of-your-pet/looking-after-your-pet/small-pets/choosing-the-right-small-pet
Learn more about whether a hamster is the right pet for you.

www.bluecross.org.uk/pet-advice/top-10-tips-looking-after-hamster
Discover ten top tips for looking after a hamster!

Index